Judy Moody's

Way Wacky Uber Awesome Book of <u>More</u> Fun Stuff to Do

Megan McDonald   illustrated by Peter H. Reynolds

CANDLEWICK PRESS

Meet Judy Moody!

Nicknames: Judy Muddy
                    Mad Molly O'Maggot
                    Madame M

School: Virginia Dare School

Grade: 3

Teacher: Mr. Todd

Principal: Ms. Tuxedo

Moods: More than she can count!

And now introduce yourself....

Name:

Nickname(s):

School:

Grade:

Teacher:

Principal:

Favorite Mood:

Name That Mood!

Check out these *uber*-awesome, brand-spanking-new Judy Moody moods:

- Wishing-for-snow mood
- No-school-today, sleep-in mood
- Stay-up-all-night-reading mood
- I-like-math mood
- Rhyme-time mood
- Declares independence mood
- I ♥ college mood
- Dance-like-a-spider mood
- Not-talking-to-Stink mood
- Mad-Molly-O'Maggot pirate mood

Can you think of another mood for Judy? What would it be called? Draw a picture of Judy in that mood!

Judy Moody, the Queen of Moods

Ten Things That Put Judy Moody in a Good Mood:

1. When her mood ring turns purple
2. Playing fake-hand-in-the-toilet jokes on Stink
3. Doctoring broken dolls
4. Getting her picture (not elbow) in the newspaper
5. Having her initials on the Wall of Gum
6. Doing yoga (not yogurt) with Mouse
7. Saving the world, one Band-Aid at a time
8. Going on a treasure hunt
9. Eating Screamin' Mimi's ice cream
10. Being a member of the My-Name-Is-a-Poem Club

What puts *you* in a good mood?

1.

2.

3.

The Game of Judy

Judy Moody gets to play the Game of Life with her math tutor, Chloe. **If you don't own the board game, don't worry—just create your own game!**

What you'll need:

- a large piece of plain paper
- crayons or colored markers
- one die
- game pieces (small pieces of colored paper, pebbles, or pieces of candy—whatever is handy will work.)

Draw a snaking line from one end of the paper to the other, or in any shape you wish. Along the line, draw circles about the size of a quarter every one to two inches. Mark one circle with the word START and one with the word FINISH.

Color in the circles or decorate the board game in whatever way you wish.

Now you're ready to play A Day in the Life of Judy Moody! The rules are:

- If you roll a 1, you are Stuck Forever in Third Grade and do not advance.
- If you roll a 2, you've been *Stinked*: Stink has played a trick on you and you have to miss a turn.
- If you roll a 3, you get a "Good Job" sticker from Mr. Todd (of Class 3T) and get to move ahead 3 spaces.

- If you roll a 4, you catch someone littering and get to move the player of your choice back 2 spaces.
- If you roll a 5, you become famous and get to take another turn.
- If you roll a 6, you get a math tutor. Multiply by 2 and advance 12 spaces!

There's no end to the possibilities. Make up your own games and your own rules, using one rule for each number on the die. You could even create A Day in the Life of You!

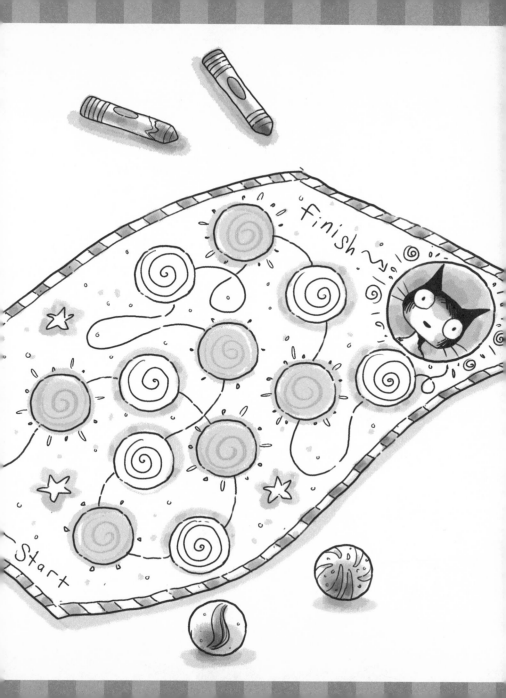

 # Ha! Fooled You!

April Fools' Day is Judy's birthday, but she likes to play jokes on Stink ANYtime of year. **Try these funny jokes on your family and friends!**

The Case of the Runaway Candy Bar

Tie a long piece of clear fishing line around your brother's or sister's favorite candy bar. Leave the candy bar in an obvious place where they'll be sure to find it. Holding the other end of the fishing line, hide behind a chair or sofa and wait. As your brother or sister reaches for the candy bar, tug on your end of the fishing line and pull the candy away!

Musical Cereal Boxes

Open all the boxes of cereal in the cupboard. Switch the inner bags around, putting the cereal from one box into a different box. When your family reaches for Lucky Charms, they may get Raisin Bran!

Hey! There's a fly on my toothbrush!

Take the cap off of the tube of toothpaste in the bathroom and push a small dark raisin into the neck of the tube. Then wait for your brother or sister to brush their teeth, and listen for the scream! When they squeeze out the raisin, they'll think a creepy-crawly got into the toothpaste!

International Fools

In Portugal, kids toss a handful of flour at their friends on April Fools' Day!

In Scotland, an April fool is called an April *gowk* (cuckoo bird)!

In England, if a trick gets played on you, you're a "noodle"!

Have
you
met
Stink?

Meet Stink, Judy Moody's little "bother," er, brother. <u>Very</u> little brother. . . .

Stink was short. Short, shorter, shortest. Stink was an inchworm. Short as a . . . stinkbug!

Stink was the shortest one in the Moody family (except for Mouse, the cat). The shortest second-grader in Class 2D. Probably the shortest human being in the whole world, *including Alaska and Hawaii.* Stink was one whole head shorter than his sister, Judy Moody. Every morning he made Judy measure him. And every morning it was the same.

Three feet, eight inches tall.
Shrimpsville.

Excerpt from *Stink: The Incredible Shrinking Kid*

Take the Personality Quiz!

**Are you more like Judy or more like Stink?
Take the test and find out!**

If you found a fake hand in the toilet, you would most likely

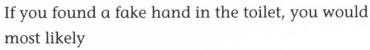

    a) laugh your pants off
    b) scream and run

If you couldn't have a two-toed sloth for a new pet, you would get a
    a) hamburger-eating Venus flytrap
    b) rescued guinea pig

You would rather sleep in a
    a) bunk bed
    b) race car bed

If you were done with your homework, you would then most likely
    a) make a Me collage
    b) read the *S* encyclopedia

For your school picture, you would
    a) leave your hair wild and messy
    b) spike your hair

The worst smell you can imagine is
   a) smelly sneakers
   b) a corpse flower

If you went on a trip, you would visit
   a) the Wall of (ABC) Gum in California
   b) a Gross-Me-Out exhibit at the museum

If you could join a club, it would be
   a) The My-Name-Is-a-Poem Club
   b) The Short-People-Rule-the-World Club

Your favorite flavor of Screamin' Mimi's ice cream
would probably be
   a) Rain Forest Mist
   b) Coconut Snowstorm

If you chose more a answers than b answers, you are more
like Judy. If you chose more b answers than a answers, you
are more like Stink. *Same-same!*

If you chose the same number of a and b answers, then you
need a math tutor!

Write Your Own Piggyback Song!

To write a piggyback song, take a song everybody knows and change the words to make it sound silly or funny (or smelly). Here's an example to get you started:

Real Song:
Old MacDonald had a farm,
E-I-E-I-O!
And on that farm he had a
* cow.*
E-I-E-I-O!
With a moo, moo here
And a moo, moo there
Here a moo, there a moo,
Everywhere a moo, moo.
Old MacDonald had a farm,
E-I-E-I-O!

Piggyback Song:
My new teacher had a cage,
E-I-E-I-O!
And in that cage she had a
* guinea pig.*
E-I-E-I-O!
With a wee, wee here,
And a wee, wee there,
Here a wee, there a wee,
Everywhere a wee, wee.
My new teacher had a cage,
E-I-E-I-O!

Real Song:
Jingle bells, jingle bells,
Jingle all the way.
Oh, what fun it is to ride
In a one-horse open sleigh!

Piggyback Song:
Jingle bells, Stink sure smells,
His sneakers are P.U.
He hasn't washed in seven
  weeks,
And his socks smell worse
  than poo!

Now try making up your own piggyback song. Use a song you know, like "Three Blind Mice" or "Twinkle, Twinkle, Little Star." The sillier your new version, the better!

Let It Snow, Let It Snow!

Judy stays up late one Christmas Eve to make sure that Stink has snow for Christmas. **If you can't make it snow for real, try making this Judy Moody–style snowflake. When it's finished, you will discover something that Judy likes to eat!**

You will need

⊚ A square piece of thin paper (origami paper works great!)

⊚ A pair of scissors

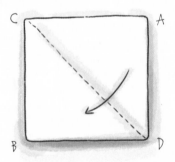

1. Fold the top right corner (corner A) of your piece of paper down to the bottom left corner (corner B), creating a triangle.

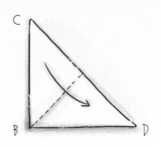

2. Fold point C down to point D. You should still have a triangle, but it will be smaller.

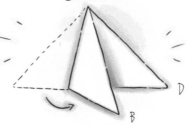

3. Fold corner B partially to the right so that the corner sticks out past the bottom edge of the triangle.

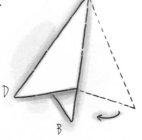

4. Now fold in the opposite corner. You should now have a tall thin triangle that looks something like a swallow's tail.

Turn the triangle over and, using the straight edge of the paper above the tail as a guide, cut across that edge, snipping off the two points of the "tail." The triangle you have left is now ready for the snowflake pattern.

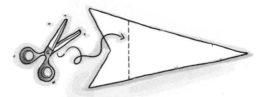

5. Draw the pattern shown onto your folded piece of paper, making sure that your lines touch an edge.

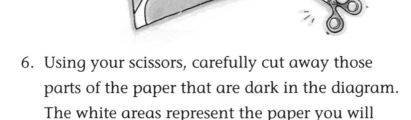

6. Using your scissors, carefully cut away those parts of the paper that are dark in the diagram. The white areas represent the paper you will have left (the snowflake).

7. When you have finished cutting, very carefully unfold the paper. Ta-da!

Amaze Your Friends!
Walk Through Paper!

Hold up a plain old 8½ x 11 inch sheet of paper and tell your friends that you can walk through that piece of paper. Chances are pretty good they'll say something like, "No way!" Then you can say, "Way!" and you can show them how:

1. Fold the plain old 8½ x 11 inch sheet of paper in half lengthwise (hot-dog fold).

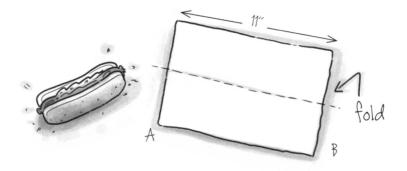

2. Starting one inch from the short end of the folded paper, cut six slits along the folded edge, stopping one inch from the other short end. The slits should be evenly spaced about 1¾ inches apart and about 4 inches long.

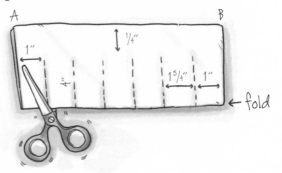

3. Starting inside the first slit, cut along the folded edge, stopping when you reach the last slit.

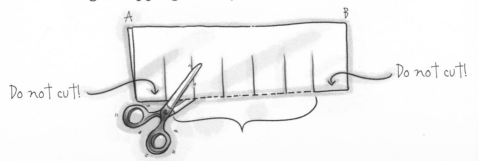

4. Turn the paper over and cut five more 4-inch slits, spacing them so that they fall between the slits on the opposite side.

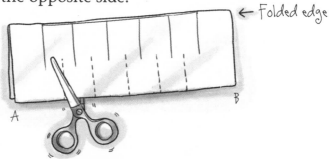

← Folded edge

5. Now carefully unfold the paper and stretch it out. You should have a ribbon-like loop or hole that's big enough to step through.

6. Step into the loop, like you're stepping into a Hula Hoop, then pull it up over your hips, body, shoulders, and head. *Voilà!* You just walked through a piece of paper!

Track Down the Moody-est Pets on the Planet

The Moody pets are running wild around the house. **Can you match each pet to its tracks?**

1) Mouse the cat

2) Toady

3) Newton

4) Sparky the dog

5) Astro the guinea pig

6) Iguana

7) Pig

8) Cookie the parrot

a)

b)

c)

d)

e)

f)

g)

h)

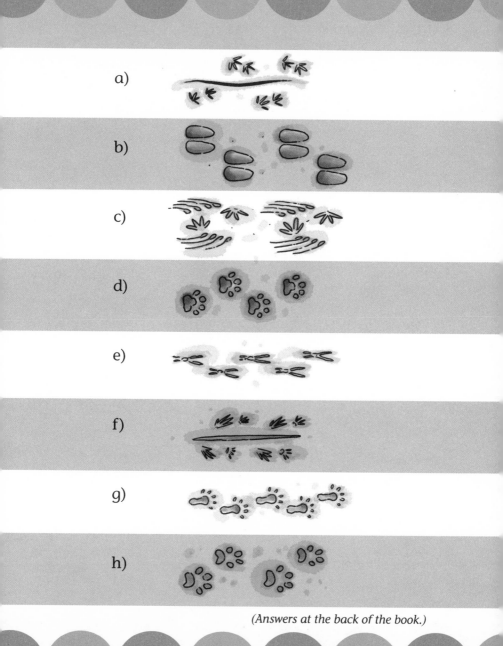

(Answers at the back of the book.)

Yoga-Not-Yogurt Poses

Try these poses for a more peaceful you.

Cat Pose

1. Get down on your hands and knees.
2. Arch your back like a cat.
3. As you let out a deep breath,
   let your back come down and relax.

Tip: Ask your brother if he'll bring you
a bowl of milk.

Cobra Pose

1. Lie face down on the floor, palms flat and in line with your
   shoulders. Inhale.

2. As you exhale, slowly lift your head and chest up off the
   floor.

3. Continue to lift, face forward, palms and hips pushing into the floor. Hold for five seconds.

4. On your next inhale, slowly lower your body and forehead back down to the floor.

Tip: No hissing allowed!

Tree Pose

1. Start in a standing position. Carefully balancing on one foot, slide your other foot up along the opposite leg until it's resting just above the knee.

2. Fold your hands in front of your chest with palms touching.

3. On your next inhale, raise your hands up over your head, palms together.

4. For 10–15 seconds, be a tree! Try not to blow in the wind.

5. Now carefully return to the standing position and try this on the other foot.

Tip: Do not try this after riding a roller coaster!

Mountain Pose

1. Stand with your feet hip-width apart, toes straight ahead.

2. Let your arms hang straight at your sides.

3. Keep your face, your neck, and your shoulders relaxed.

4. Imagine a straight line going from your feet up through your spine to the top of your head. You're a mountain!

Tip: Stink uses this pose as an anti-shrinking device.

What's in Your Pack?

In 1889, news reporter Nellie Bly set off on a trip around the world, aiming to do it in less than eighty days. She packed light—only one small piece of luggage (16 inches wide and 7 inches tall) into which she fit two hats, three veils, a pair of slippers, toiletry articles, an inkstand, pens, pencils, paper, a small sewing kit, a bathrobe, a blazer, a flask and a cup, a few changes of underwear, some hankies, and a jar of cold cream. Oh, and she brought along some money, too.

What five things would you pack for a trip around the world if you could only bring one bag no bigger than your backpack?

1.

2.

3.

4.

5.

Around the World in ~~80~~ 72 Days

Nellie Bly made her trip around the world in seventy-two days, six hours, eleven minutes, and fourteen seconds traveling by ship, train, and burro, and beating Phileas Fogg, the fictional hero of Jules Verne's novel *Around the World in Eighty Days.*

Now it's your turn! Be a world traveler. If you turn the page, you'll find a map of the United States showing its different time zones. Test your mad math skills and find out what time it is all over the place.

1. Jack Frost, the Moody family's mail carrier, spends every Christmas in Alaska, which is four hours behind Virginia, where Stink and Judy live. If Jack gives Stink a call at 9:00 PM on Christmas night to wish him a Merry Christmas, what time will it be in Virginia when Stink answers the phone?

2. Two kids—one who lives in Hawaii, the other who lives in western Kentucky—love the Judy Moody books. Both of them begin reading *Judy Moody Goes to College* on the very same day, April 1, at 7:00 PM. So which of the kids starts reading the book *first*?

3. Scurvy Sam the Pirate lives on Ocracoke Island, North Carolina, but his mom, Scurvy Samantha, lives on Key West, Florida. Will Scurvy Sam have to change the time on his watch when his visits his dear old mom?

4. Judy Moody is on her way from Virginia to Screamin' Mimi's in California. If she stops in Ohio, Minnesota, Colorado, and Nevada on the way, how many different time zones will she have visited by the time she reaches the ice-cream shop?

Using the map, try making up your own questions to ask friends and family!

(Answers at the back of the book.)

U. S. Time Zones

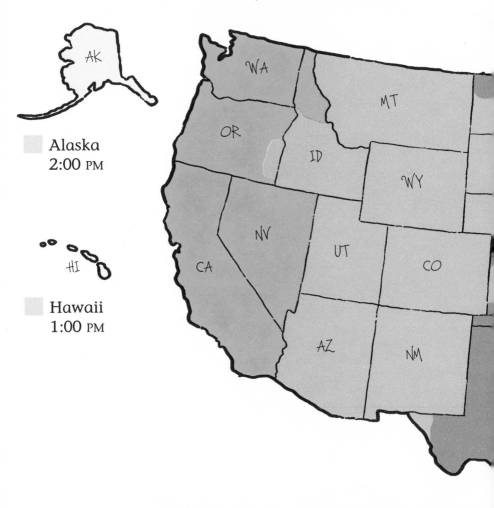

Alaska
2:00 PM

Hawaii
1:00 PM

Pacific
3:00 PM

Mountain
4:00 PM

ND

MN

WI

MI

IL

OH

PA

NY

ME

NH
VT
MA
RI
CT

SD

IA

IL

E

KS

MO

KY

WV

VA

NJ
MD
DE
DC

OK

AR

TN

NC

TX

LA

MS

AL

GA

SC

FL

Central
5:00 PM

Eastern
6:00 PM

Aloha!

 *Aloha* means "Hello" on the islands of Hawaii. Here's how to say "Hey" (Hello) and "Later" (Good-bye) in other languages:

	Hello	Good-bye
Arabic	*Salaam*	*Maasalaama*
Chinese (Mandarin)	*Ni hao*	*Zai jian*
French	*Bonjour*	*Au revoir*
German	*Guten Tag*	*Auf Wiedersehen*
Hebrew	*Shalom*	*Kol Tuv*
Hindi	*Namasté*	*Alavidha*
Japanese	*Konnichiwa*	*Sayonara*
Korean	*Annyong ha shimnikka*	*Annyong hi ka shipsio*
Latvian	*Sveiki*	*Uz redzesvanos*
Portuguese	*Bom dia*	*Adeus*
Russian	*Privyet*	*Do svidaniya*
Spanish	*Hola*	*Adiós*
Swahili	*Jambo*	*Kwaheri*

Say Bonjour to Fleur Humeur

Judy Moody has been published in more than ten languages! Here are some of Judy's other names.

Serbia:	Caca Faca
Poland:	Hania Humorek
Netherlands:	Fleur Humeur
Slovakia:	Dada Nalada
Hungary:	Durrebele Dorka

My Name Is a Poem

When Judy Moody meets Amy Namey, they join a club for people who have names that rhyme, like:

Hugh Blue
Newton Hooton
Sing Ling
Larry Derry Berry
Viola Gazola
Lance France

Roos Van Goos
Wong Fong
Nathaniel Daniel
Mark Clark van Ark
Chip Dippe
Nancy Clancy

Join The My-Name-Is-a-Poem-Club!

Write your real first name here:

Now make up a new last name that rhymes with it:

Write your real last name here:

Now make up a new first name that rhymes with it:

Judy Moody Is a Hinky Pinky!

A hink pink is two one-syllable words that rhyme, like *fat cat*. Since *Judy Moody's* two names are *two* syllables and rhyme, it's called a hinky pinky! Can you guess the answers to these funny hink pinks?

Where does Judy Moody's little brother like to ice-skate?

What do you call a frog's dirty diaper?

What would you call rules for Judy's Venus flytrap?

Where does Judy Moody's cat live?

What do you call a joke played on Judy's friend who eats paste?

(Answers at the back of the book.)

Moodily We Roll Along

Don't let a long car trip put you in a nark! Whether you're rollin' down the highway on a road trip or swervin' and curvin' in your own car bed, don't leave home without some Judy Moody books and some car games!

The Way-Fun JUDY MOODY License Plate Game

See if you can find mentions of each of these states somewhere in a Judy Moody or Stink book:

Alaska	Newt Hampshire
California	New York
Connecticut	North Carolina
Hawaii	Pencil-vania
Maine	Rhode Island
Massachusetts	Vermont
Maryland	Virginia
Minnesota	Washington, D.C.
New Jersey	

BONUS: Win a dollar if you can find any of the above Judy Moody states on a real license plate! Turn to the back of the book for your dollar!

The Cow-culator

You will need at least two players or two teams. Each player or team chooses a side of the road. Set a limit in time, miles, or length between rest stops. Start counting cows! Each player or team gets one point for every cow they see on their side.

DEAD COW ALERT!
If you spot a cemetery on your opponent's side and yell, "Your cows are dead!" they lose all their points and have to start over.

Bump up your score with these awesome bonuses:
10 points:
tractor, water tower, bridge, hawk, chicken, sheep
25 points:
pizza sign, ice-cream truck, kite, school bus, airplane vapor trail
50 points:
white horse, clown, hot-air balloon
100 points:
rainbow
1,000 big ones:
dog with an eye patch, person dressed as pirate, life-size Venus flytrap, albino alligator, billboard with the word *Pneumonoultramicroscopicsilicovolcanoconiosis*

Can't-Stump-Me Riddles

RIDDLE ONE

In marble walls as white
  as milk,
Lined with a skin as soft
  as silk,
Within a fountain
  crystal clear,
A golden apple doth
  appear.
No doors there are to
  this stronghold,
Yet thieves break in and
  steal the gold.
What am I?

RIDDLE TWO

Lives in winter,
Dies in summer,
And grows with its root
  upwards.
What am I?

RIDDLE THREE

Thirty white horses upon a
  red hill:
Now they tromp,
Now they chomp,
Now they stand still.
What am I?

RIDDLE FOUR

I weigh less than a feather,
but no one wants to
carry me.
What am I?

RIDDLE FIVE

I dance in white from head
  to toe.
The warmer it gets, the
  faster I go.
Snap . . . crackle . . . POP!
What am I?

(Answers at the back of the book.)

RIDDLE SIX

What has a mouth but can't eat, a bank but no money, a bed but never sleeps, and waves, but has no hands?

RIDDLE SEVEN

What occurs once in a minute, twice in a moment, but never in a day?

RIDDLE EIGHT

I'm a shiny, bright dragon, Breathing fire all the while. I'll eat up your breakfast And give it back with a smile.

What am I?

RIDDLE NINE

I huff and I puff. I may blow down your house. But if you look me in the eye, I'm quiet as a mouse.

What am I?

RIDDLE TEN

I'm a tiny yellow sun. I smile and I sway. One night I'll turn white, And my hair will blow away.

What am I?

RIDDLE ELEVEN

I'm tall and I'm yellow. Hold me tight. Let me get to the point: The longer I go, The shorter I grow.

What am I?

Driving Judy Crazy

TPCLUB

I ♥ TOADY

IM MOO D

I 8 SHARK

OOHLALA

STINKR

IOU MULA

JUDY M D

RARE X 2

So what if you can't drive! **Design your own license plate.** You can use letters, numbers, or both—but no more than seven in all!

Mood Libs!

Get in the mood to write your own Judy Moody mini-mystery!

One _____ and _____ night,
       adjective   adjective

Judy Moody, Stink, and _____ were
                                 name of person

home alone. The wind outside _____
                                    verb (past tense)

and rattled the _____. Inside, without
                 part of a house

warning, the lights _____ once and
                      verb (past tense)

then went out. Suddenly, Judy, Stink, and

_____ heard a _____
  same person   adjective

_____ down in the _____.
    sound   room

They _____ downstairs. They looked for a
     verb (past tense)

_____. They heard a creak and a
  scary creature

_____, and then the door slammed shut
sound

with a _____.
loud noise

Stink screamed, "_____," and
screaming word

grabbed Judy's _____. "C'mon, let's get
part of the body

outta here!" he screeched.

"We have to go down into the _____.
same room

What if Mouse is _____?"
verb (-ing form)

"OK. You go first," Stink whispered.

Judy tiptoed down the hall and opened the

_____ _____. Long _____
adjective   part of house   scary adjective

shadows fell across the stairs.

_____, went the steps on their
scary sound

way down. It was as dark as _____.
noun

Stink held his breath. _____
same person as before

picked his/her nose. Judy _____ turned
adverb

the knob on the closet door.

All three closed their eyes.

"_____!" When they opened their
screaming word

eyes, out _____ not Mouse, not Toady,
verb (past tense)

but _____!
monster/creature/dinosaur

Rub-a-Dub-Rub

Judy and Stink like to make rubbings of old
gravestones. **Here's how to make a crayon
rubbing of just about anything:**

- Peel the paper wrapper off of a crayon.
  Choose any color.
- Find something with texture and place it under
  a blank piece of paper.
- Using the side of the crayon, rub it across the
  blank paper over the bumpy object several times.

Here are a few ideas for textured objects to get you
started:

leaves	keys
coins	lace
corrugated cardboard	brick
paper clips	bubble wrap

How to make a fish or a dragon rubbing:

- Save the netting from a bag of produce (such as oranges or potatoes).
- Place a plain piece of paper on top of the netting.
- Rub the side of a peeled crayon across the paper over the netting to make it look like scales.
- Now draw an outline of a fish or a dragon on the scaly paper.
- Cut out your work of art and hang it on your fridge Hall of Fame.

Meet Mr. Todd!

These are some of Judy's favorite things about her teacher, Mr. Todd:

- Gives out Thomas Jefferson tricorn-hat stickers
- Wears groovy glasses and a crayon tie
- Mood ring turns red when he wears it
- Cares about endangered species
- Does not have an Attitude Tent

- Good listener
- Helps save the world (one recycled bottle at a time)
- Takes Class 3T on field trips
- Does not get mad when Judy tries to clone guinea pigs

Name three things that make your teacher special:

1. Shes nice

2. Shes nice

3. Shes nice

Field trip! List three places you'd like to go:

1. hallos fome

2.

3.

Pasta Match Game

While working on her Italy project, Judy learns that there are lots of names for pasta.

Can you match each pasta shape to its name?

1) Rotini

2) Elbow macaroni

3) Farfalle

4) Penne

5) Spaghetti

6) Ziti

7) Ravioli

a)

b)

c)

d)

e)

f)

g)

(Answers at the back of the book.)

Other Cool Pasta Names

Many pastas are named after what they look like. Some of the Italian words can be translated into English!

Anellini ("Little rings")
Campanelle ("Bells")
Cappelletti ("Little hats")
Cavatappi ("Corkscrews")
Conchiglie ("Shells")
Ditalini ("Little thimbles")

Gemelli ("Twins")
Manicotti ("Muffs")
Orecchiette ("Little ears")
Radiatori ("Radiators")
Rotelle ("Little wheels")
Farfalle ("Butterflies")

Use Your Noodle

If you could design your own pasta, what would it look like? Draw a picture of it here. What would you name it?

hello kitty Bow

Sticky Business

Fun Facts about Chewing Gum

- Gum is made from chicle, which comes from the sapodilla tree.
- Native Americans chewed resin from spruce trees.
- Susan Mont"GUM"ery Williams blew the biggest bubble-gum bubble ever—23 inches!
- Only 2 percent of fourth graders can blow a double bubble—a bubble inside a bubble.
- A triple whammy is when a person blows a bubble in a bubble in a bubble!

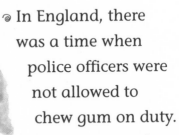

- In England, there was a time when police officers were not allowed to chew gum on duty. The gum might get stuck if they had to blow their whistles!

"Pop" Quiz

1. The oldest piece of gum ever discovered was:
   a) 150 years old
   b) 500 years old
   c) 9,000 years old

2. Which country makes the most gum?
   a) Turkey
   b) China
   c) the United States

3. The oldest piece of gum on the real wall of gum in Bubble Gum Alley in San Luis Obispo, California, is:
   a) less than 5 years old
   b) 25 years old
   c) almost 50 years old

4. The very first bubble gum, invented by Frank Henry Fleer in 1906, was called:
   a) Fiddle-faddle
   b) Blibber-blubber
   c) Double Bubble

(Answers at the back of the book.)

Spoonerisms!

Judy Moody and Stink star together in a book called *The Holly Joliday*. But it's backward! They meant to say *Jolly Holiday*. When letters get mixed up, it's called a spoonerism.

Here are a few more spoonerisms:

> Lack of pies   *(Pack of lies)*
>
> It's roaring pain   *(It's pouring rain)*
>
> Wave the sails   *(Save the whales)*
>
> Fight my liar   *(Light my fire)*
>
> Go shake a tower   *(Go take a shower)*
>
> Chip the flannel   *(Flip the channel)*
>
> Here comes the pun fart   *(Here comes the fun part)*
>
> I think I hit my bunny phone   *(I think I hit my funny bone)*
>
> I like belly jeans
>
> *(I like jelly beans)*

Guess what these funny spoonerisms say:

a) teepy slime

b) chilled greese

c) well-boiled icicle

d) a dot in the shark

e) flutter by

f) tuna lick

g) your stocks sink

h) let's go to the mood fart

i) a scoop of boy trouts

j) parrots and keys

k) spork, fife, and noon

(Answers at the back of the book.)

Test Your Judy Moody IQ

1. What's the name of Judy and Stink's new mailman?
    a) Santa Claus
    b) Jack Frost
    c) the Hulk

2. When Mr. Todd takes a trip, who is Judy's new substitute teacher?
    a) Mrs. Grossout
    b) Mrs. McGross
    c) Mrs. Grossman

3. What's the name of Judy's college tutor?
    a) Chloe
    b) Bethany Wigmore
    c) Chelsea

4. Where does the substitute teacher send Judy for a time out?
    a) Antarctica
    b) the Attitude Tent
    c) the flagpole

5. What costume does Stink wear to dress up
   for the 10th Annual Holly Joliday Holiday
   Happening?
   - a) Mouse
   - b) a human flag
   - c) a stellar dendrite

6. What dance does Judy have to dance all by
   herself when her friends are mad at her?
   - a) the triceratopia
   - b) the tarantella
   - c) the tappatula

7. What does Judy stay up half the night making
   for Stink on the night before Christmas?
   - a) marshmallow snowmen
   - b) star-shaped cookies
   - c) paper snowflakes

8. What's in the mysterious package that arrives
   on Christmas Eve?
   - a) fruitcake
   - b) a Yule log
   - c) red-and-green mittens

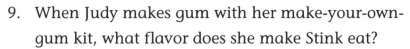

9. When Judy makes gum with her make-your-own-gum kit, what flavor does she make Stink eat?

    a) pizza gum

    b) ketchup-and-mustard gum

    c) Pickle Chicle

10. What does Judy write her miles-long Christmas list on?

    a) toilet paper

    b) paper towels

    c) her bedroom wall

11. What nickname does Judy give Stink when she is learning some Italian words?

    a) *finkarino*

    b) *ratioli*

    c) *bratellino*

12. What do Judy and Tori, her friend from England, collect together?

    a) tea bags

    b) sugar packets

    c) stamps with queens on them

13. What event do Judy, Rocky, Frank, and Stink celebrate in the Moody's upstairs bathroom?
    a) the Boston Tub Party
    b) the Boston Toilet Party
    c) the Boston-Cream-Pie Party

14. What is Stink's favorite attraction on the Freedom Trail in Boston?
    a) Mother Goose's grave
    b) Paul Revere's house
    c) the musical toilet

15. What award does Stink think Judy won for her college painting?
    a) Horrible Mention
    b) Messiest Painting Ever
    c) Pop-Eye Pop Art Award

16. What does Judy write on her tie-dye shirt she makes at college?
    a) PEAS ON EARTH
    b) PEACE IS POPSICLES
    c) PEACE IS CRUCIAL

17. In college speak, what does NCP stand for?
   a) Nincompoop
   b) Nerdy College Person
   c) Nice Cool Penguin

Super-Duper Way-Real-Hard All-Time Brainy
Bonus Stumper:

What's Judy's address in Virginia?
   a) 170 Toad Pee Way
   b) 117 Croaker Road
   c) 107 Mood Mansion Lane

Give yourself a point for each correct answer.
Answers can be found at the back of the book.
Add up your points to get your score!

You are a Judy Moody:

0–4	**Newbie**	
	(Time to read some more Judy Moody books!)	
5–10	**Bordering on Brainiac**	
	(Has read a few Judy Moody books)	
11–15	**Triple A++ Super-Smart**	
	(Has read most Judy Moody books)	
16–18	**Double-Rare World's Expert**	
	(Has read them all and can't wait for more!)	

Flip Out Over Flip-Flops

Flip-flops are an important part of Judy's college style. **Show off your own style by decorating a plain pair of flip-flops. Pick your favorite colors, or accessorize them to match a special outfit.**

- You'll need a pair of flip-flops with plastic straps.

- Using ribbon or strips of fabric, cover the plastic straps by wrapping the ribbon or fabric around them. Use a few drops of hot glue to keep the ribbon or fabric in place.

- Then it's time to get creative! Use sequins, beads, buttons, glitter, puffy paint, or whatever else you'd like to make your flip-flops one-of-a-kind. You can even try small shells, gemstones, or fake flowers. Use hot glue to attach your accessories.

Double-rare tip: Use your leftover decorations to make a matching hair accessory. Use hot glue to attach sequins, flowers, glitter, or other decorations to a plain headband or barrette.

Extreme Room Makeover

When Judy visits the local college, she is inspired
by her tutor's radical dorm room to go home and
"college up" her own room. Are you tired of
looking at the same four walls, the same stuff day
after day? Sometimes it's good to shake things up
and change things around.

**Here are a few simple things you can do to
make your room seem like a whole new universe:**

- Create a new attitude! Move the furniture around.
  (Ask an adult for help.)
- Take down your current wall decorations
  and replace them with all new stuff. Try new
  posters, your own artwork, a Me collage, paper
  snowflakes, etc.
- Create a color scheme or theme and try to use
  it on your bed, pillows, desk, rug, and wall
  hangings. Your theme could be the rain forest or
  outer space, the beach, or even pink pigs!

- Paint the walls. Even painting one wall a different color can change the look of your space to way-cool. Go purple! (Remember to ask the 'rents for help!)
- Go through all your stuff and store or give away things that you don't use anymore. You could even hold an *uber*-rad yard sale.

★ ★ ★ ★ ★ Pop Art ★ ★ ★ ★

Make a Popular, Eye-Popping Work of Art

When Judy Moody goes to college, she learns to make a pop-art painting like Andy Warhol.
To make your own pop art, you'll need:

A pencil
A thin piece of styrofoam (from an art supply store; or you can use a produce tray from the supermarket with the edges cut off)
Tempera paint
A shallow tray or cookie sheet
A small paint roller, or brayer
Paper

★ ★ ★ ★ ★ ★ ★ ★ ★ ★ ★ ★ ★ ★ ★ ★ ★ ★ ★

◎ With the pencil, draw a simple line picture on the piece of Styrofoam. Make sure you press down evenly and hard enough so that the lines are carved, or "etched," into the surface, but not so hard that you puncture it.

◎ In the same way, "etch" a name or any other letters or words on the Styrofoam. If you do this, remember to write your letters and words backward! R A R E!

- Pour some paint into the tray or cookie sheet. Dip your roller or brayer into the paint and roll it back and forth until it's evenly and thinly covered, not dripping.

- Pull the paint-covered roller back and forth across your Styrofoam etching until it's completely and evenly covered. (Be careful that the carved lines of the drawing don't fill up with paint.)

- Carefully place a blank sheet of paper across the Styrofoam's painted surface.

- Gently rub your hand across the back of the paper to make sure the paint sticks evenly to the other side.

◉ Lifting the paper by two corners, carefully peel
it away from the Styrofoam and lift it up. *Voilà!*
Your masterpiece.

Now change colors! First wash the Styrofoam plate
and dry it. Then roll it with a new color. Line the
prints up side by side or one on top of the next or
in a square or other shape. See how great they look
together!

After your prints dry, don't forget to sign them!

VOF (Very Own Fridge)

After Judy went to college, she wanted a pink mini fridge in her room. If you had a mini fridge, what would you keep in it?

A milkshake?
An apple?
A penguin?
Some tie-dyed Jell-O?
Worms?
Leftover pizza?
A science project?
Popsicles?
A frozen banana?

Fill the fridge with pictures of your favorite cool things.

What does your fridge say?

Choose from the words below to make your own way-wacky sentence on Judy's fridge:

moody   musical   super-galactic
way-cool   purple   toilet
spaghetti   undies   jawbreaker
smelly   rare   same-same   fake
hand   bother   roar   dictionary
in love   hairy   tarantula
screamed   mood ring   fink
teacher   bunk bed   pizza   yelled
paste   toad   shrinking   attitude
friend   grouchy   very   stink
Jaws   eats   Band-Aid   pj's
ouchy   brother   best   likes
pickle   bad   snowflake   sang
un   ooh-la-la   *uber*   shark
for-real   operation   broken
three-headed   of   is   he   she
am   was   and   we   our   for
they   you   it   them   ran   has
over   such   in   a   the   went
my   his   her   their   from

What does Judy's fridge say?

Way-Not-Boring, Un-Baby Math Games

Judy Moody has E.S.P. (Extra Special Powers). You can have it, too! **Amaze your friends with this way-cool math trick!**

- Tell your friend to pick a number between 2 and 9. (2 and 9 are OK, too.)

- Ask them to multiply their number by 9.

- Their number should be two digits. Tell them to take the two digits and add them together. (Example: For 39, add 3 + 9 to get 12.)

- Tell them to subtract 5 from that number. Match that new number to a letter of the alphabet. 1=A 2=B 3=C 4=D 5=E 6=F 7=G 8=H 9=I

- Now tell them to think of a country that begins with that letter (such as Argentina for *A* or Bulgaria for *B*).

- Now have them take the second letter of the country and think up an animal that begins with that letter (such as aardvark for *A* or bear for *B*).

⚙ Ask your friend if they are now thinking of a country and an animal.

⚙ Now tell them you need to concentrate. (Act like you're thinking really hard.)

⚙ Now say, "I didn't know there were elephants in Denmark!"

⚙ Watch the look of amazement on your friend's face.

Pizza Par-ty!

Judy, Rocky, Frank, and Amy each ate a different kind of personal pizza for lunch. After lunch, there was: ¼ cheese pizza left

⅓ pepperoni pizza left

½ mushroom pizza left

⅝ ham-and-pineapple pizza left

Judy ate the most. Rocky ate the least. Frank ate more than Amy. What kind of pizza did each kid eat?

(Answers at the back of the book.)

The Ups and Downs of College Life

Judy went to college to visit Chloe, her tutor. On the first floor of Chloe's dorm is the lobby, elevators, game room, and TV room. Floors 2–6 are for male students, and the top five floors are for female students.

Judy visits Chloe, who lives on the floor that is second from the top. Chloe's friend Paul is playing the drums six floors down, and Judy goes down to hear him. In a little while, she gets hungry and goes to find a vending machine. The vending machines are four floors above the lobby.

Chloe's roommate, Bethany Wigmore, is hanging out in a friend's room that is three floors above the vending machines. Judy takes a candy bar up to Bethany. What floor does she end up on?

(Answers at the back of the book.)

Math Jokes

Why did Judy Moody take her Women of Science ruler
to bed?
Answer: *She wanted to know how long she'd slept.*

If two's company and three's a crowd, what's four and five?
Answer: *Nine.*

Why did Mr. Todd sit on Judy Moody's new watch?
Answer: *He wanted to be on time.*

Why did Mr. Todd wear sunglasses to school?
Answer: *Because his class was so bright.*

Why did Judy Moody throw away her math book?
Answer: *It had way too many problems.*

What did Stink write his book report on?
Answer: *Paper.*

Why did Stink put his money in the freezer?
Answer: *He wanted cold, hard cash.*

The Uber-Rad, Sick-Awesome Judy Moody Word Search

Can you find all of these words about Judy hidden in this puzzle? Draw a line through or a circle around each word when you find it.

ABC GUM

ALOHA

BALONEY

BLACKBEARD

BRATELLINO

COOL YULE

CRAB

GECK

HOGSHEAD

JACK FROST

KIMO

MOUSE

OLD SKOOL

PEEPS

PIRATE

PUNCH BUGGY

RAD

TOAD PEE

UBER

```
B  M  O  K  E  A  M  E  G  P  B  T
M  L  C  L  H  T  L  O  U  N  R  S
U  E  A  O  D  U  A  N  U  T  A  O
G  P  L  C  Y  S  C  R  O  S  T  R
C  A  O  L  K  H  K  A  I  P  E  F
B  Y  O  M  B  B  D  O  E  P  L  K
A  O  O  U  I  P  E  E  O  T  L  C
C  H  G  G  E  K  P  A  Y  L  I  A
Y  G  Z  E  A  S  B  A  R  C  N  J
Y  H  O  G  S  H  E  A  D  D  O  W
M  A  S  Y  V  R  U  C  S  D  A  R
S  Y  E  N  O  L  A  B  U  B  E  R
```

(Answer at the back of the book.)

Make Your Own T-Shirt

Judy got to make her own tie-dye T-shirt at college. **Here's a simpler way of making your own glad rag!**

You'll need:

- a plain white T-shirt (half-cotton, half-polyester blend)
- a drawing of Judy Moody (provided at the back of the book)
- a pencil
- black puffy fabric paint
- an iron
- washable crayons

1. Copy the picture of Judy Moody onto the T-shirt with a pencil.
2. Go over the pencil lines with the black puffy fabric paint.
3. When the fabric paint is dry, turn the T-shirt inside out and go over the drawing with an iron.

4. When the T-shirt has cooled, turn it right side out and color in the picture of Judy with washable crayons.

5. Each time the T-shirt is washed, the colors will disappear and you can color Judy again!

(Wash the shirt separately in hot water with regular detergent and no bleach to prevent the colors from getting onto your other laundry.)

Peace Is Crucial

When Judy Moody visited college, she got to be part of a peace rally. Peace begins with Y-O-U! **Give peace a chance!**

Send Peace Around the World

- Cut several lengths of ribbon or strips of paper into 18-inch pieces.
- Write a personal message or wish for peace on the paper or ribbon. (A few ideas are listed below if you're having trouble coming up with your own.)
- Go outside and tie the ribbon onto the branch of a tree.
- Let the wind carry your wishes, dreams, and hopes for peace around the globe.

Peace Starts with Me
Save the World
Peace Is the Answer
Pull Together for Peace
Peace Is Crucial

Be a peacenik!

Write an acrostic poem for peace here:

P_____

E_____

A_____

C_____

E_____

Start a Peace Garden

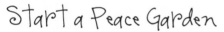

A garden is a quiet, peaceful place. Planting a
garden connects you with other people and the
planet. **Start a peace garden by planting a few
seeds or plants.** Sunflowers and roses are symbols
of peace. What else can you add to your garden to
give it a peaceful feeling?

Imagine "Whirled" Peace

Join over one million people in 3,000 places spinning pinwheels for peace. Create a pinwheel and start spinning!

☮ Start with a piece of paper that's square (like origami paper) or cut a piece of paper into a square.

☮ Starting at each corner, make a cut toward the middle, stopping about one inch from the center.

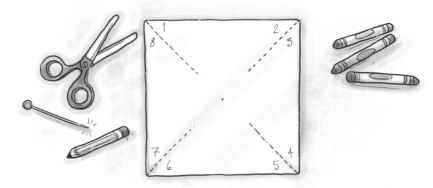

☮ Fold corners 1, 3, 5, and 7 into the center.

☮ Hold the pinwheel in place with a straight pin at the center.

- Poke the end of the pin into the eraser on the end of the pencil.

Time for spin class! Go outside and watch your pinwheel spin in the wind.

September 21 Is International Peace Day!

Ask your teacher or principal if an announcement can be made to celebrate a Peace Minute on September 21. Turn off all computers, cell phones, guinea pigs, and anything else that makes noise in the classroom. At noon, invite everybody in the whole school to stop what they are doing. Take one minute of silence and imagine peace around the world. At the end of one minute, invite everyone to join in saying together, "Peace is possible."

PEACE OUT!

Flip Out Over Flip Books

Change Judy Moody's mood!

1. Grab a pencil and a sticky-note pad.
2. Start with the bottom sheet, and draw Judy's frowning face in the lower right-hand corner.
3. Turn to the next page (second-to-bottom) and draw Judy's face again. This time, move it up and to the left of the one you drew before.
4. Draw her face over and over. With each page, move her face (just a little) to a new spot, and change the expression slightly. Little by little, turn Judy's frown into a smile.

6. Now flip through all your pictures. Watch your friends flip out as they sit back to enjoy the show.

Tip: Think up some of your own ideas, or flip out on making a flower grow, a ball bounce, a flag fly, or Judy ROAR!

Wish List

Judy Moody's Ultimate *Uber*-Rare Wish List

Pink mini fridge

Not-candy cell phone

World Peace

World's coolest Band-Aid collection

Better spelling

To be a doctor, like Elizabeth Blackwell

Stink had un-smelly sneakers

Mood ring to turn purple

Bring back the endangered northeast beach tiger beetle

Save the rain forest

Stink Moody's Suberbad,
Super-Rad Wish List

Stop shrinking and grow taller

Snow for Christmas

Newton would come back from the drain

Find a REAL moon rock

Pockets full of money

More free stuff in the mail

Smell a corpse flower

Grow up and get job as professional smeller

Be a superhero

Meet James Madison

Make a wish! Write your ultimate *uber* wish list here:

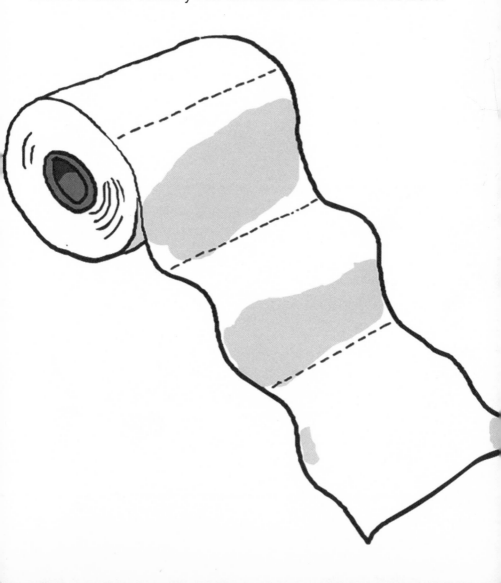

10 Things You May Not Know About Megan McDonald

10. The first story Megan every got published (in the fifth grade) was about a pencil sharpener.

9. She read the biography of Virginia Dare so many times at her school library that the librarian had to ask her to give somebody else a chance.

8. Megan had to be a boring-old-pilgrim every year for Halloween because she has four older sisters who kept passing their pilgrim costumes down to her.

7. Her favorite game to play is the Game of Life.

6. She is a member of the Ice-Cream-for-Life Club at Screamin' Mimi's in her hometown of Sebastopol, California.

5. She has a Band-Aid collection to rival Judy Moody's, including bacon-scented Band-Aids.

4. She owns a jawbreaker that is bigger than a baseball, which she will never, ever eat.

3. Like Stink, Megan had a pet newt that slipped down the drain when she was his age.

2. Megan often starts a book by scribbling on a napkin.

1. And the number-one thing you may not know about Megan McDonald is: she was once the opening act for the World's Biggest Cupcake!

10 Things You May Not Know About Peter H. Reynolds

10. He has a twin brother, Paul. Paul was born first, fourteen minutes before Peter decided to arrive.

9. Peter is part-owner of a children's book and toy shop called the Blue Bunny, located in the Massachusetts town where he lives.

8. He's vertically challenged (aka, short!).

7. His mother is from England, and his father is from Argentina.

6. He made his first animated film while he was in high school.

5. Peter sometimes paints with tea instead of water— whatever's handy!

4. Peter keeps a sketch pad and pen on his nightstand. That way, if an idea hits him in the middle of the night, he can jot it down immediately.

3. His favorite candy is a tie between Reese's peanut butter cups and Raisinettes (same as Megan McDonald!).

2. One of his favorite books growing up was *The Tall Book of Make-Believe* by Jane Werner, illustrated by Garth Williams.

1. And the number-one thing you may not know about Peter H. Reynolds is: he shares a birthday with James Madison, Stink's favorite U.S. president!

Experience all of Judy's moods.

MEGAN McDONALD #1

JUDY MOODY

was in a mood

illustrated by Peter H. Reynolds

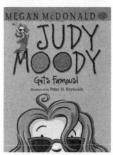

MEGAN McDONALD #2

JUDY MOODY

Gets Famous!

illustrated by Peter H. Reynolds

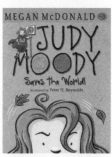

MEGAN McDONALD #3

JUDY MOODY

Saves the World!

illustrated by Peter H. Reynolds

MEGAN McDONALD #4

JUDY MOODY

Predicts the Future

illustrated by Peter H. Reynolds

Be sure to check out Stink's adventures, too!

☐ Stink: The Incredible Shrinking Kid

☐ Stink and the Incredible Super-Galatic Jawbreaker

☐ Stink and the World's Worst Super-Stinky Sneakers

☐ Stink and the Great Guinea Pig Express

☐ Stink: Solar System Superhero

Answers & Templates

LET IT SNOW! TEMPLATE:

MOODY-EST PET TRACKS
1d, 2c, 3a, 4h, 5g, 6f, 7b, 8e

HINK PINKS
A Stink rink
A toad load
Jaws laws
In a Mouse house
A Frank prank

AROUND THE WORLD
1) It will be 1:00 AM on December 26, the day *after* Christmas
2) The kid who lives in western Kentucky starts reading first because when she starts, it won't be 7:00 PM on April 1 in Hawaii for another four hours!
3) No! They both live in the eastern time zone.
4) Four: Virginia and Ohio are in the eastern time zone (1); Minnesota is in the central

time zone (2), Colorado is in the mountain time zone (3), and Nevada and California are in the pacific time zone (4).

RIDDLES

Riddle One: An egg
Riddle Two: An icicle
Riddle Three: Teeth
Riddle Four: Mosquito
Riddle Five: Popcorn
Riddle Six: A river
Riddle Seven: The letter *M*
Riddle Eight: A toaster
Riddle Nine: A hurricane
Riddle Ten: A dandelion
Riddle Eleven: A pencil

PASTA MATCH

1d, 2b, 3f, 4c, 5g, 6a, 7e

POP QUIZ

1c) 9,000 years old
2a) Turkey
3c) almost 50 years old
4b) Blibber-blubber

SPOONERISMS

a) sleepy time
b) grilled cheese
c) well-oiled bicycle
d) a shot in the dark
e) butterfly
f) lunatic
g) your socks stink
h) let's go to the food mart
i) a troop of boy scouts
j) carrots and peas
k) fork, knife, and spoon

JUDY MOODY IQ

1b, 2c, 3a, 4b, 5c, 6b, 7c, 8c, 9c,
10a, 11c, 12b, 13a, 14c, 15a,
16c, 17a
Brainy bonus stumper: b

MATH GAMES: PIZZA PARTY

Judy ate the cheese pizza.
Rocky ate the ham-and-pineapple pizza.
Frank ate the pepperoni pizza.
Amy ate the mushroom pizza.

Draw your BONUS DOLLAR here:

MATH GAMES:
UPS AND DOWNS

Chloe lives on the 10th floor
(there are 11 floors and she is
second from the top).
Paul drums on the 4th floor.
The vending machines are on
the 5th floor.
Bethany Wigmore is hanging
out in a room on the 8th floor.

WORD SEARCH

```
B  M  O  K  E  A  M  E  G  P  B  T
M  L  C  L  H  T  L  O  U  N  R  S
U  E  A  O  D  U  A  N  U  T  A  O
G  P  L  C  Y  S  C  R  O  S  T  R
C  A  O  L  K  H  K  A  I  P  E  F
B  Y  O  M  B  B  D  O  E  P  L  K
A  O  O  U  I  P  E  E  O  T  L  C
C  H  G  G  E  K  P  A  Y  L  I  A
Y  G  Z  E  A  S  B  A  R  C  N  J
Y  H  O  G  S  H  E  A  D  D  O  W
M  A  S  Y  V  R  U  C  S  D  A  R
S  Y  E  N  O  L  A  B  U  B  E  R
```

T-SHIRT FACE TO TRACE: